Mikka Mi Amor

(Mikka My Love)

by
Bones Kendall

BBC

Originally, these poems were sent, in 2003, as emails accompanying pictures borrowed from the Internet. In some cases, the pictures helped to generate ideas for the poems. That nature of being able to share is what has inspired me to not want to protect all of my rights regarding your use of these poems.

Visit www.MikkaMiAmor.com

Copyleft 2007
BBC, PO Box 803, Whittier, CA 90608

Evan "Bones" Kendall asserts the moral right to be identified as the author of this work.

Any use, reuse, or reproduction (not-for-profit) IS ACCEPTABLE where credit to the author is given.

That means YOU CAN FREELY COPY ANY OF THE POEMS so long as Bones Kendall is noted as the author.

For-profit rights will most likely be granted; just ask.

ISBN: 978-0-9798934-0-7

How to Use This Book / Frequently Asked Questions

Will this book help improve my love life and/or my English?
- That is its intent.

How will it help help improve my love life?
- Read the first half of this book containing fifty poems representing love, dedicated to love, and written with love on the brain; they celebrate romance, the impulse to feel good, and the complications of love.
- Give a copy of the book to loved ones and see what happens.

How will it help improve my English?
- The second half of this book contains my definitions for every word used in the poems. That way readers can quickly flip to the back to learn the meanings of words they might not know. Learning words in context is better than rote memorization. Reciting them will help even more.
- Most of the poems contained within use meter and rhyme.

    In most, but not all cases, I went for exact rhymes, meaning the pronunciation is the same as the matching word, so if one line ends with "stare" the next line might end with "care". Other types of rhymes that I tried to avoid are close but not exact, for instance, "Vegas" with "outrageous", which don't rhyme exactly.

    The goal of meter is many, but it is also to help non-native speakers "hear" the sound patterns in English. It's the musical quality readers should hear in their heads when reading the poems or sounding them out. This part can be especially hard for non-native speakers. Practice by reading them aloud.
- If you have a computer, check out www.MikkaMiAmor.com

How should I read the book, straight through?
- The poems are not sequential. Skip around if you like.

The poems are to Mikka, but is "you" always Mikka?
- "You" is whomever you wish it to be. It's your imagination that gives them meaning. Meaning is what you bring to the words you read.

Contents

Foreword..........................3
Poems.........................7 – 107
Afterword.....................108 – 110
<u>Glossary</u> (handmade definitions of words used in the poems)..............111 – 160

7	What can a poem do?
9	I love my wife more
11	I get my inspiration from a muse.
13	Last night you and I did some kissing,
15	I have a muse
17	My teacher never told me
19	Throughout the ages–
21	So what if my verse is corny.
23	A frog alone cannot play.
25	You are like a poem to me–
27	You fog up my glasses,
29	You shouldn't fall in love with what you begin,
31	If you want to know
33	I hope I never forget the bliss
35	My girl's like a terrier.

37	When my baby feels sick
39	In her bathroom lair,
41	I do
43	What can I do to be more romantic?
45	Sometimes my bones feel like dancing
47	Do you remember when we went to Vegas?
49	There's something nebulous about us–
51	There's been a problem at home
53	I missed you last night
55	Last night was my birthday dinner.
57	Quick, look up! What do you see?
59	(The Blank Poem – Mikka's Favorite)
61	Against you I like to rub.
63	Yesterday I didn't feel much like
65	I've got my web cam on you.
67	Let's play monkey together!
69	You didn't get a poem yesterday.
70 – 71	I hate poetry.
73	Some say I write really bad poems.
75	I've got to get the meanness out of my head,
77	When I'm late to work,
79	I don't know anything.
81	I like it when my baby's naked.

83	your purple hair
85	Mi amor, tengo algo que decirte–
87	If you happen to be a friend of Freud
89	Here is a little something odd but new–
91	It's Sunday morning and the countdown has begun–
93	My paradise would not exist without her
95	If I were a rockstar,
97	Love is less about what's inside our hearts
99	Hit me with poetry! & Bomb me with verse!
101	When you lie naked on the bed
103	When we're together
105	Her fragrance
107	When the lights are down low

Foreword

To Mikka, my love: I'm too poor to give you diamonds. I'm too poor to give you a new car, a fancy vacation, designer clothes, money or just about anything material.

All I have are the feelings inside my heart and the words I can string together...but maybe these are more valuable...and, who knows, if we're lucky, they might stand the test of time.

Skip This Page

To the Reader: I wanted to add to this book some kind of critical justification for why it's not just a simple collection of poems by a poet about a specific subject. But then I asked myself what's wrong with it being such a simple collection of poems. I have no good answer, so then I have no real need to write the boring critical justification about semiotics, metaphor, metonymy... And besides, I really tried to include the critical justification within the poems themselves.

Since these are mostly love poems, I do hope that those who know understand that I'm attempting to position myself within the tradition of young poets who write about love. My intention, though, which may differ from many of my contemporary peers, is to write poetry that is fun to read. Why? Because so little poetry is actually read by folks these days that I figured maybe it's the fault of the poets who write stuff that's too academic, abstruse or otherwise mostly unreadable.

I'm humble about this, though. While I'd love to prove that poetry is supposed to reach out to the audience rather than demand that the audience be literate enough to get it, really I'm just a guy who is not afraid to be a lover. So as a lover, let my words inspire you to love. If I fall short, let my words inspire you to try to do more. You never know, perhaps you are the next great person who uses words to express things that exist beyond simple comprehension.

What can a poem do?

Ask the professor who studies Homer,
Or a medieval bard roamer
Who went around wooing
Using fine words pursuing.
Or ask the African griot
To tell you what he knows.
They will all answer with glee
For they are all fans of poetry.
If you're a bit younger don't be shy,
Talk to a rapper, go ahead and try.
Preserving poetry is up to us,
So climb aboard the magic bus.
Verse can take you from here to there,
Some other time, or anywhere–
Riding high on the wings of metaphor
Is what lies in store–
And it's where you, too, can be,
If you learn to appreciate poetry.

I love my wife more
Than I love my
Pocketknife.
That's saying a lot.
She's sharper,
More dangerous,
And she has more uses.

But neither one can I do without.
Luckily there's no jealousy.

I get my inspiration from a muse.
"You're so corny, that's a ruse,"
She said, making me turn red.
She's right, you know,
But I do hear voices in my head.

I draw on life for inspiration.
I notice things, like perspiration.
"Oh, no, not another lame line,"
She said–she's so smart.
But I need to practice to refine.

Inspiration often comes to me
From above. "Cheesy, cheesy,
Try again," she gently chided.
I'm not afraid, I'm a fool,
For to put my soul in verse I decided.

What can I say, what can I do?
She said "Just to yourself be true."
And so I will keep on going,
Looking up, down and around–
Seeking inspiration, but never knowing.

Last night you and I did some kissing,
And that's what I am now missing.
Making out is a fun thing to do–
Especially when it's me and you.
'Cause I don't mind tasting your spit;
Really, there's not much to it.
I silently close the lids of my eyes
And patiently wait for a surprise.
I feel you press against my lips
As my hands rest upon your hips.
There's nothing lascivious to this,
Just you and me and a simple kiss…
Or two or three more.

I have a muse
Who gives me clues
And teaches me
To write poetry.
She makes me rhyme–
To pass the time,
So my verse'll shine,
And so it doesn't read:
"Like stars and moons
across the heavens
I drift through space
On wings of an interstellar
Comet hoping I'll be carried
Home to my sweet
Love." That's lame.
Bad poetry sounds the same.
Sure, my verse may be worse
But difference is what I choose.
I blame it on my muse–
She's my delightful curse.

My teacher never told me
That poetry is play.

When there is no game,
When you're stuck somewhere lame
With nothing to do,
And you start to feel blue–
There is one thing
That I recommend,
But you have to have
Paper and pen,
Or perhaps a computer.
It's not masculine,
Feminine or neuter.
It's poetry and
It's a form of play.
Don't be afraid
Of being called gay.
Just pass the time
Writing rhymes,
And you shall see
What fun it can be.

Mikka Mi Amor

Bones Kendall

Throughout the ages,
Across the sea that rages—
Like well worn stone
Or fossilized bone—
Our love is here to last.
It started in the past
And goes on to the future.
You and I, fused together
Like skull bones in a suture.
Staying close, as if tethered
We are; each a part of the other.
Believe it; I have no doubt.
Get me up high and I'll shout
To my sisters and brothers,
For all to hear, close and near—
"We shall unite to persevere!"
And that's it. But it's not the end.
For long after our final breath,
Outliving even death,
Our love will continue...

So what if my verse is corny.
It's all a big lie.
I'm just really horny
And you caught my eye.
See, when I look at you
There are things I want to do.
You make me feel awkward.
I want to express my emotion,
But doing it out loud causes commotion,
And you tell me to be quiet.
So I'm restricted to verse.
What would you rather read,
Something corny or terse?
Let go of censure.
Laugh if you want.
Mock if you please.
Just don't lead me on
Or be a tease.
I put my heart on the page,
And by your reaction I gauge
What works and what fails.
Don't take the wind out of my sails.
Corny it may be,
But baby, that's the season.
Horny I am,
And baby, you're the reason.

Leapfrog

A frog alone cannot play.
He hops by himself all day,
Never getting very far,
Always wishing upon a star
For a playmate.

Flashforward two years.
The frog has no more fears.
Into his life came someone new,
And that frogette is you.
You're first rate.

You are like a poem to me—
Delib'rately imperfect unity.
Not quite pure, but near,
An error in meter here,
A line that's not quite straight,
Rhymes that aren't quite great,
A hair that's out of place,
And an all too human grace.
Yet somehow the details conspire
To make that of which I don't tire.
Unique it is and so are you—
A vessel which if true
Is bursting with emotion.
I live through my devotion.
There may be a finer beauty
Or poems that have more formal duty,
But if there were no faults,
You wouldn't be you,
And what I want this poem
To say wouldn't be true.
You are my purposely—or is it purposefully—
Imperfect poetry.

You fog up my glasses,
And laugh at my passes.
You are filled with mirth.
I'll make you give birth
To a love that will grow—
So get ready, get set, go!

You shouldn't fall in love with what you begin;
You should only feel love for that which you end.
The risk is lust which is a deadly sin.
It's only love when lust you transcend.
What's so important about this lesson?
Love is forever, not just a session.
It may be hard to deny lust's motion,
But would you rather a wave or an ocean?
It's the small and selfish versus the vast—
If you do it the right way it will last.
Lust will come again and go don't you know;
Better to take your time and go real slow.
Because feeling love is something you earn,
Not just that for which all of us do yearn.

If you want to know
Why the poems I write you aren't deep—
I'm trying not to put you to sleep!
They don't contain the wrath of Plath
Or the strange song of Whitman.

I just want to write you from my heart—
A few lines, nothing too smart.
I suppose they could be darker like Parker,
Or cloistered like Dickenson—

But they're not. My sole poetic intention
Is to write happily, by convention.
We're not in the woods, lost like Frost,
Or anguished like Ginsburg.

I'm simply writing simple poems to my girl
Who puts my head in a whirl,
And I'm thankful I'm not Eliot.

I hope I never forget the bliss
Of your lips and mine
Locked in a kiss.
When we make out
I am transported.
I forget myself.
I feel exported
To another country.
Are you on the same flight?

My girl's like a terrier.
She thinks that makes
Me scared of her,
But really I don't mind.
She's pretty cute
Most of the time.
Piss her off, though, and she growls,
Furrows her brow and scowls.
I only wish I could be a better
Best friend.

When my baby feels sick
I try to be quick.
I warm a bowl of soup
And toss in a flick.
I climb into bed
And caress her head.
"I love you,"
To me she said.

In her bathroom lair,
My baby does her hair.
She plucks her eyebrows
With incessant care.
And when she dresses,
She impresses,
But it doesn't cost a lot.
She shops vintage.
I don't know where she gets it from,
But she definitely beats a different drum.
I may be wrong, but I will say
That she's the face of the new LA.
I don't mind that it takes her a while–
It's all worth it to me,
'Cause my girl's got great style.

I do
Not want to crawl into your bed.
I want to climb into your head.
Not because I'd get to look back at me,
But because there's so much to see.
I'd spend endless fascinating hours
In countless nooks and secret bowers,
Wondering why you do the things you do,
Trying to guess what's a lie and what's true.
I'm dying to know what you think about—
When you're sure and when you have doubt.
I'd be happy if I could only discern
What it is that makes you yearn.
But how can I fit into so small a space?
It's not possible…unless I'm already there.

What can I do to be more romantic?
Not much, you see, I'm too pedantic.
Somebody out there, help me!
I'm about as amorous as irony.

But if I were a different man,
I might not have such difficulty.
I would try as hard as I can—
Risking it all, even penalty,
Just to sweep you off your feet,
To give to you a special treat,
To be a man that can't be beat.
Yes—
I would cross the sea in a desperate race
To once more lay eyes on your pretty face.
I would swim to the bottom of the ocean
To impress you with my deep devotion.
I would spend my life trying to teach
If I thought it could bring us within reach.
I would dedicate to you a book of poetry
Just to try and get you to sleep with me.

I really wish I knew how to romance,
But I don't even know how to dance.
The only thing I can do to get a date
Is prevaricate.

Sometimes my bones feel like dancing.
Occasionally they're into romancing.
Sometimes I am not so elated.
Please don't think my love is overrated.
But since we have united,
We haven't really fighted,
And that's what makes me happy.
I feel myself dripping with sappy,
So I'll shut up now and won't bug your ear
With all the things you don't want to hear.

Que nos entierren juntos.

Do you remember when we went to Vegas?
The time we had was downright outrageous.
I don't remember us having any fights,
And I can still see you under the downtown lights.
In the room we had on the thirtieth floor,
Lots went on behind the closed door.
It was so new. I was still nervous,
But we stayed up late and got room service.
And shortly after that time
I knew that you would be mine.

There's something nebulous about us—
Ethereal, celestial and contradictory.
Yet no one I know can doubt us,
For we are real and not a story.
I am tall and you are short
So let me be your umbrella.
I promise not to laugh and snort
When Tommy-boy calls you Cruella.
All across this vast thing called space
I think of you and your pretty face,
And I think about us mixing race,
Which is pretty cool, at least in our case.

There's been a problem at home
So today you get a special poem.
Yesterday you didn't really moan.
You were strong, almost like stone
Despite the loss of the baby–
We can try again soon, maybe.
But for now, think of what might've been–
A baby with no eyes, no face, no chin.
Or perhaps we would have had a rat,
Certainly nothing cute like a cat.
Maybe the baby would have had fur,
Or perhaps it would have been a cur.
You know, I'm glad we lost the fetus.
Sure it's sad, but it won't defeat us
Because we already sail in the same boat
And we will again unite in a zygote.
This poem doesn't seem to want to end.
As in life, there's more around the bend,
And that's what we're supposed to learn–
To be together through every twist and turn.

I missed you last night
at four in the morning.
I arose from deep slumber
without any warning.
I had to go pee.
It was very cold you see,
And when I climbed
back into bed,
I shivered and said,
"Warm me up mi amor, please."
But you weren't there–
Only your scent lingered, to tease.
Dammit! It's true, I need your care–
For in the winter months you can't be beat
'Cause my skin and bones generate no heat.

Last night was my birthday dinner.
We ate so much, neither of us is thinner.
Delicious it was, but not quite stocky,
Like my all time favorite, sukiyaki.
If bean curd is me and cabbage is you,
Then let's simmer together in a stew.
I'll cook the meal and to you I'll cater,
But don't forget, it's always better a day later.

Quick, look up! What do you see?
It's a couple of squirrels
running through the tree.

What if they were you and me?
With our beady little eyes
What would we see?

There, in the window, is it me and you?
No furry bodies? No bushy tails?
Lying in bed all day, nothing to do…

How foreign then would be our life?
For if we were squirrels,
You would not be my wife.

Perish the thought! For I have this to say,
If we were tree-dwellers,
I'd share my branch with you any day.

(The Blank Poem—Mikka's Favorite)

Against you I like to rub.
Feed you, I do, with grub.
Tousle your hair–
Enter your lair–
And never let you go.

Be with you I will
'Til we die and still
More if I could.
I feel like I should
At least try and let you know.

Yesterday I didn't feel much like writing poetry.
There was no rain.
I was in no pain.
I felt no joy.
Never once said, "Oh boy."
It was normal beyond belief,
And I just wanted some relief.
Something dramatic.
A little bit of static.
Excitement would fit the bill,
Anything but staying still.
Alas, no luck was in store for me,
Not until I got home eventually.
But then it was too late.
I had missed the date.

I've got my web cam on you.
I see all that you do.
It's a little jumpy at times
And a little fuzzy are the lines,
But you always shine through.

Let's play monkey together!
We can do it in any kind of weather–
Hot or cold, young or old.
Break the mold. Let's be bold!
I'll pop your zits, you pop mine–
Soon we'll be feeling fine.
'Cause it's not just about kisses and hugs–
I'm not afraid of your bacteria or bugs.
I just want you to know I care
And that I'm not afraid to share.
I'm writing this poem and when I'm through
I want to go home and play monkey with you.

You didn't get a poem yesterday.
At first I thought that was bad–
But I had nothing to say,
And I realize now that I'm glad.
For if I had written you a poem
It wouldn't have been about
What I saw when I got home,
Which was amazing, no doubt.
Just in case you didn't know,
We live in warm Los Angeles,
So to see a sled without snow
Borders on miraculous.
But sure enough my eyes did spy
A boy sliding down the stairs.
He didn't drop from the sky,
And he didn't have any cares.
He was riding on a pillow sled
Followed by Marsi giggling.
Laughter turned their faces red,
And their little bodies were jiggling.
You and I joined in the fun–
Such was the pleasant setting.
Finally this poem is done.
I dedicate it to sledding with bedding!

I hate poetry.
There isn't a thing about it I like.
Ever since I stopped being a kid.
Hating poetry is what I did.
When I was a teenager I thought it was stupid–
Oooh! Look, another poem about cupid.
Yawn, belch and fart!
That's no work of art.
And when I left to go to school,
I still didn't think poetry was cool.
I met the Romantics and
My opinion didn't change.
This tree, that tree on a greenish hill.
It still makes my stomach turn.
But then I met the Age of Reason–
Though passed, it seemed a cool season
To be alive, to prosper and thrive,
But into poetry I did not yet dive.
I had, by then, practiced some rhyme,

But I didn't give poetry any time.
When I switched from reading to writing
Maybe I learned a thing or two more,
But poetry still was not inviting–
Little did I did know what lay in store.
I'll be damned if I weren't as stiff as wood
When I felt that piercing arrow's prick–
Hold on, that metaphor's not so good,
'Cause really you landed on me like a brick.
Then I was caught in the muse's spell–
I guess it's just as well,
For I found the poet within
The castle of my skin.
So I dedicate to you these firsts
Of my poetic outbursts
Because it's all because of you
That hating poetry I no longer do.

Some say I write really bad poems.
They say I shouldn't even write prose.
Well I might not be a scribe of tomes,
And my meter might not smell like a rose,
But what a rose is keeps on changing,
And history is made in rearranging.
So even if I just make waste,
I shall keep on doing it with haste.
I don't want to brag at all.
I just want you to like my doggerel…
Now let's go have a bacchanal!

I've got to get the meanness out of my head,
So I'll turn my thoughts to you instead.
While I sit here at work smirking at the jerk,
I realize in my choler that I do have one perk.
I'd like to say it's you, but I won't ever tell–
Because then your head will grow big and swell
with air–how funny you would then look–
This sounds like something I read in a book.
"Balloonhead! Take me with when you fly away,
Because I really do not want to be here today."

When I'm late to work,
I'm afraid to say why,
But at home there's a perk,
Which just makes me high.
How can I walk out the door
Without a smack of the lips?
How can I cross the floor
And not glance at those hips?
Believe me, this isn't seduction—
There's not enough time.
But neither is it production,
And they say that's a crime.
However, I take another view—
I'm not afraid of the dare;
In fact, I challenge them to
Place a value on care.

I don't know anything.
Birds sing, dogs bark.
I try and write poetry.
A chorus of voices can steer
My direction and I'll get lost.
I'm so dense I don't know fear
And believe me, that costs.
There's just one thing
That I overstand–
It's less about the ring
Than about the hand.

I like it when my baby's naked.
No denying it, I can't fake it.
But this isn't an elaborate con.
There's nothing wrong going on.
I don't buy into someone else's shame.
I'm trying to play a different game.
There are too many plastic images
Trying to infiltrate my desire.
I'm not looking for beauty
When my baby's naked,
I'm looking for truth.
Besides, what do you think
She sees when I'm unclothed?
Imperfections are special-tease.

your purple hair
    it makes them stare
        but you don't care.
you like to dare.

they see your face
    and guess your race
        it's no disgrace.
you just outpace.

it's like a book
    the way you look
        but you're no crook.
baby, you cook!

you're not on a stage
    or locked in a cage
        you're on my page.
now let's engage!

Mi amor, tengo algo que decirte—
If I live to see past this day,
Away we'll go, muy lejos.
Pero, the hour now is close.
There is a task at hand—
I have to go matar a man.
Es por honor—
Say nada more.
Hear the beat of the drum,
And smell tequila and rum.
I sense the enemy is close—
In battle, I know I'm feroz.
As the gun fight begins,
For fear, I repent my sins.
Y cuando viene la jura—
If God grant me ventura,
I will be the one standing.
They can be demanding,
But all I'll say is I did it
Para ti, Mikka mi flor.
Recuérdeme siempre—
Soy tu bandido del amor.

If you happen to be a friend of Freud
You might believe in his theory,
Or, at least, you might have a query
About our desire to re-enter the void
From which we all came–otherwise called the womb.

It goes a little something like this:
Since our mind's first sensation
Happens during the nine-month gestation
When we are in a state of unknown bliss,
It's to there we all desire to return…subconsciously.

But you can't take the doctor literally.
For instance, when my lady and I are in bed–
Lying under the comforter which is red,
It could be like a womb, metaphorically.
I think this is what I was supposed to learn in class.

It's been a long, eight or more year quest,
And now I can finally find some relief
From that Austrian man and his beliefs.
So with this poem I happily put to rest
All my thoughts and troubles about this subject.

Baby, now that that's out of my head,
Why don't we spend the rest of the day in bed?

Here is a little something odd but new—
Instead of it being from me to you,
I'm writing this poem a different way,
So I'm trying to guess what you would say.

Will you tell me how safe I make you feel?
Or how you can't resist my macho appeal?
Doubt it. How about a nice compliment
About how you're driven wild by my scent?

I should know better. You've got too much sass.
You flatter me by calling me an ass—
My legs are skinny and I've got no butt—
In high school, I wouldn't have made the cut.

These digs and others you often repeat,
But I know you know for you I can't be beat.

It's Sunday morning and the countdown has begun–
Hold on tight, we're about to have some fun.
Tennineeightsevensixfivefourthreetwoone–
Blast off!
The engines thrust and we are on our way.
We've got nothing to do all day today
Except stay in bed and play play play!
In our spaceship we travel far and wide–
Across the seas and over mountains we glide.
In the whole universe this is my favorite ride.
Our timeship lets us witness history,
Keep up with the news, and solve mysteries.
So many people, animals and sights to see–
Just you me and our bed's window to the world…
The TV.

My paradise would not exist without her
But there's only room for one.
That's my pesky paradox.
I'm a fool 'cause I fell for a fox
Who says just a word and it's done.
You might say it's a high price to pay
But fate wouldn't have it any other way.
Adrift you'll often find me,
In the green garden of my gray matter,
Until I hear Eve call–
It's when I rush to respond
That I trip and fall.
She laughs with mirth and
I'm learning to as well,
Because my paradise only exists
When I am under her spell.

If I were a rockstar,
Would you be my backstage girl?
After I finish the set,
Finish cursing at the world–
I'd climb off stage
Ready to rage.
There you would be waiting
Among the others
You put to shame.
'Cause compared to you,
They're all the same.

Because I'd be famous,
I'd be on MTV–
And then all the girls
Would fall for me.
But you won't be jealous,
You won't even accuse,
Because you know damn well
That you are my muse.
And by the way,
If I were a rockstar,
I would not drive a fast car.

Mikka Mi Amor — Bones Kendall

Love is less about what's inside our hearts
And more about sharing each other's farts.
Or sometimes because of the late hour,
If one of us doesn't take a shower,
The other one can get a little whiff
Of an aroma that can be quite stiff.
Sometimes I catch you without warning
With my stinky breath in the morning.
It's true, smelly pits are a fact of love–
The earthly kind, not the kind from above.
Believe me, it might not make too much sense,
But for the record, this poem's my two cents.
You wanna know how I know I love you?
For me no one else's b.o. will do.

Hit me with poetry!   &   Bomb me with verse!
When I feel rage   There is no repose
I pound hard on the keys   I can't stop creating
To print on the page   Poetry or prose
Something to outlive the age!   My appetite—it just grows!

Club me with rhyme!   &   Beat me with meter!
The ball I won't drop   I want to be the best
My method is serial   I take on any challenge
Tell it to a cop   I can withstand any test
I want to rise to the top!   And I won't ever stop.
                                         No, I won't ever rest!

When you lie naked on the bed
In the Saturday morning light,
More than words run through my head–
Oh delight! It's such a sight.
Your back is like a painted canvas
With the promise of an exotic locale;
And when I see the other side
I know that you're my erotic gal.
So let's stay in bed all day today
And communicate without words
All the things we don't have to say,
Just like the bees and the birds.

When we're together,
It's like I'm on drugs.
Instead of little pills,
Give me kisses and hugs.
Face it, I'm addicted.
I can't just say no.
If you launch a war
My desire will grow.
Read between the lines
Because I'm about to snort–
Ahhhh! I feel strong,
Stronger than a fort!
So feed my habit
Because here's the thing,
When I'm high on you,
I feel like I'm the king!
What's my regalia?
You are…
My legal paraphernalia.

Her fragrance
Makes me dance
She puts me in
A trance

Her sweet smell
Makes me swell
I'm under
Her spell

Her pheromones
Make me moan
Exerting strength
I groan

Her fine scent
Is my event
Tired now
I'm spent

When the lights are down low
And you want to hear a poem,
You give a tug on my big toe,
And out comes a red-capped gnome.

"What can I do for you?" he asks.
"Would you like me to recite?"
It's in your glory he basks–
His one hope, to bring you delight.

Say yes and he'll do as you wish–
He'll even give it away for free.
'Cause he likes eating from your dish.
He's the magnificent gnome of poetry!

If you laugh or cry at his words–
You'll give him immense pleasure.
His verse as pretty as the singing birds–
Your satisfaction will be his measure.

He don't care what's proper and prim,
He hates what's reprehensible,
The only thing that disgusts him
Is when poetry is inaccessible.

Afterword

    My name is Evan Kendall. My wife, to whom this collection is written, nicknamed me Bones because I'm so skinny…and I prefer Bones to Jesus, which is another word she uses to describe me when I take off my shirt and expose my torso. I'm pale, too. When I put on a white T-shirt and walk out the door she will say: "You better go back inside and put a shirt on," or: "They won't serve you in the restaurant without a shirt."

    Ahhh…the joys of cohabitation. But I wouldn't have become a poet without her teaching me to laugh at myself. At the time I happened to work for a very serious man and I prayed daily to the gods of poetry not to turn out all serious like him.

    Speaking of work, I had a picture of Mikka on my desk and a production assistant came into my office and saw it.

    "Is that your girlfriend?" he asked incredulously.

    "My wife, actually. Isn't she beautiful?"

    "She is…man, what's she doing with you?"

    That's a good question. What is this beautiful, stylish and witty girl doing agreeing to marry a guy who would rather be an artist than be financially secure?

    The only reason I ever got from her was when she said it's because I give her butterflies in her stomach.

Now, I'm a slow guy who doesn't understand the first thing about emotions. I may have read a bunch of books, but what good are they? ("You got ripped off!" Mikka is fond of reminding me when the student loan payments are due.) She was teaching me something I knew intellectually, but not actually. I listened to her, but I didn't really understand her then. It was later, after the first year of marriage that I finally understood her metaphor for love.

Wow! What a revelation! You can express love through metaphor! I remember thinking to myself that it would get old if I kept repeating, "I love you" over and over again over the course of our lives. I knew I had to think of a better way to express how I feel and finally I understood that that's what my girl had taught me before we got married. Why did it take me so long to realize? Because so many good things take time to appreciate.

Since human beings create meaning in our lives, it is possible, over time, to turn an ordinary love into an extraordinary one. Some people buy things for loved ones; some build palaces like the Taj Mahal. Me, I write poetry. As much as I want to live a poetic life, Mikka has taught me that my life is no different from anybody else's—there are bills to pay, public restrooms to use, an employer to work for—really, the only place to live a poetic life is in language. Luckily I have a source of material unlike any other. Mikka really is my inspiration, even when she's making fun of me…especially when she's making fun of me.

Surprisingly, Mikka was kind enough to agree to let me try and sell these poems. My goal is to inspire others who seek to convey their truths not by showing off themselves, but by showing that to which they are devoted and the level at which they are devoted to it. For me, it was love that spawned these poems…even if they are all lies.

I leave you with one final anecdote: on a cold night in a small northern California community, I was standing next to a six-foot tall wooden stake serving as support for a growing sapling. A few of us were waiting for a table at a restaurant. The wind blew hard and Mikka came near me and said: "Keep me warm." If that doesn't make you laugh, let me explain. Mikka didn't hug me for warmth; instead she hugged the wooden stake, pretending to confuse it with skinny me. Resigned to my fate, I had the good sense to laugh.

Glossary

This is not a dictionary; it's just a way to help people understand some of the words I used and the way I used some of the words in the preceding poems. The author assumes no liability with regards to the preciseness of the definitions because this was hand-crafted by me. Yes, it took a loooooooong time. I originally only set out to define the less well-known words, but I couldn't resolve what is and isn't known.

This word: could mean:

A: used to indicate a single but unspecified noun; one
Aboard: get on; join in
About: referring to; close to; approximately; referencing
Above: over; on top of; heaven
Accuse: to say someone did something; to charge; to blame
Across: spanning or going from one end to the other
Admit: take responsibility for; come clean; own up; allow entrance
Adrift: drifting; floating
Afraid: scared; hesitant
African: from Africa
After: following
Again: one more time
Against: in opposition to; next to, touching
Age of Reason: as I use it, a period of English literature from 1650 to 1800; part of the greater Age of Enlightenment. Poets from the era include: Milton, Dryden, Pope and Swift. In general what I like about poetry from the period is the formality in terms of structure and also the amusing use of wit.

Age, ages: era; period of time in existence
Ahead (go ahead): proceed
Ahhhh: an expressive interjection sometimes meaning relief
Air: what we breathe; what we fill balloons with
Alas: too bad
Algo: Spanish for something
Alive: in existence
All: everything; everyone
Almost: just about; nearly
Alone: without anyone; what Bob Marley says it hurts to be
Already: happened previously
Always: eternal; every time
Am: variation of to be
Amazing: awe inspiring; full of wonder; really cool to see or do
Among: part of; in a group with
Amor: Spanish for love
Amorous: love-filled; romantic
An: variation of a
And: as well as; combined with; also
Anguished: pained; tormented; what my mother tried to make me
Animals: living beings other than plants; furry creatures; what they show on Animal Planet
Another: one additional; a different one
Answer: reply; response
Any: one or some (this is a hard word to define)
Anything: any object; or…it could also mean nothing
Anywhere: any place
Appeal: what we like; what's attractive
Appetite: what we consume; that which we hunger for
Appreciate: like; enjoy; find valuable
Are: variation of to be

Aroma: odor; smell; scent
Arose: woke up
Around: near; surrounding on all sides; on the other side of
Arrow's: belonging to the arrow, which is a long, pointy thing that shoots through the air; or a directional pointer
Art: that which makes at least one of us feel emotion
As: like; equally; the same; because
Ashamed: embarrassed; feel weird about; afraid
Ask, asked, asks: question; demand
Ass: a fool; an idiot; a jerk
At: in the same place; where something is located; general word used to indicate direction, meaning time or space
At times: once in a while
Ate: consumed by eating; dined
Austrian: from the European country of Austria
Away: somewhere else; a distant place
b.o.: body odor
Baby: a newborn child; a term of affection
Baby's: contraction for baby is; belonging to the baby
Bacchanal: a big party; a crazy party; an orgy
Back: the spine side of the human torso; the opposite of forward; behind
Backstage: behind the stage; what the audience usually does not see
Bacteria: micro-organisms
Bad: not good; (or, in a weird way: really good)
Ball: a typically round, typically inflated device used in games
Balloonhead: someone with a really big, air-inflated head
Bandido: Spanish for bandit; thief; revolutionary
Bard: a poet
Bark: a noise dogs make when they talk

Basks: enjoys; takes pleasure in
Bathroom: a room that typically has a toilet, a sink and/or a shower/tub
Battle: a confrontation
Be: exist
Beady: small and round
Bean curd: tofu
Beat: bested; topped; to pound
Beats: pounds on
Beauty: what attracts us
Because: as a result of
Becomes: turns out to be
Bed: a piece of furniture for sleeping
Bedding: sheets, pillows, mattress pads and other accessories for a bed
Bed's: belonging to the bed
Been: past tense for be
Bees: flying insects that are typically yellow and black, make honey, and sting
Begin, begins, begun: start; commence
Behind: in back of; on the other side of
Being: existing as
Belch: burp; eructate
Belief, beliefs: what we conceptualize; what we think is true
Believe: the act being convinced; to accept something as being true
Bend: curve; twist
Besides: next to; otherwise
Best: most good; highest quality
Better: superior
Between: in the middle of
Beyond: farther than; more than
Big: large

Bill: see "fit the bill"
Birds: typically refers to animals with feathers that fly; members of the Aves family of living organisms
Birth: the beginning of existence
Birthday: the day on which life begins; the annual day we celebrate a birth
Bit: a small amount
Blame: accuse; assign responsibility for or to
Blank: empty; clean of markings
Blast: an explosion; a good time
Blast off: what rockets do when they journey into space
Bliss: happiness
Blue: one of the primary colors; sad
Boat: a vessel for transport on water
Bodies: vessels which contain life
Bold: courageous; fearless
Bomb: an exploding device; to set off such a device
Bone: what makes up a skeleton
Bones: a nickname Mikka gave me because I'm so skinny
Book: a collection of writing
Borders: is nearby
Both: two together
Bottom: what's underneath
Bowers: hiding places; recesses
Bowl: a shallow container like a plate, only deeper
Boy: a male child
Brag: boast; talk up yourself
Branch: the part of the tree between the leaves and the trunk
Break: smash up
Breath: the air that goes in and comes out of living beings
Breathe: to take many breaths

Brick: a building block, typically made of clay
Bring: carry with or to
Broke: out of money; past tense of break
Brothers: male siblings; males who share the same mother and/or father
Brow: the ridge over the eyes
Bug: an insect; to bother and/or annoy
Bugs: inects; small organisms
Bursting: exploding
Bus: a large vehicle typically for transporting humans
Bushy: furry; shaggy
But: instead; except; on the contrary
Butt: the fleshy part at the rear top of the legs
Buy: purchase; believe
By: next to; because of; with the help of
Cabbage: a leafy vegetable
Cage: an enclosure typically with bars
Call, called, calling, calls: summon; refer to; name
Cam: short for camera
Came: past tense of come
Can: is able; is possible
Cannot: is not able; is not possible
Can't: contraction for cannot
Canvas: a fabric on which artists paint
Capped: hatted; worn on a head
Car: automobile; passenger vehicle
Care: comfort; extend a feeling toward; worry about
Cares: worries
Caress: a tender touch; kind petting
Carried: held; brought with
Case: situation; instance
Castle: a man's home; a fortified or otherwise protected dwelling

Cat: a feline
Catch: nab; grab and hold
Cater: provide with food; serve
Caught: past tense of catch
'Cause: short for because
Cause, causes: make happen
Celestial: heavenly
Censure: condemn; criticize
Cents: units of currency–100 in one dollar
Certainly: definitely; with exactitude
Challenge: dare; invite to compete
Change, changing: alter; deviate
Cheer: shout with glee
Cheesy: phony; cheap
Chided: lightly scolded
Chin: the frontmost part of the lower jaw
Choler: anger
Choose: pick; opt for
Chorus: a group of people singing together
Class: a group of people studying together
Climb: mount; scale; ascend; move up
Cloistered: sheltered; confined
Close: shut; near
Closed: shut
Club: beat, typically with a stick or baton
Cold: having a low temperature
Collection: grouping
Comes: arrives; shows up
Comet: a body typically composed of rock and gas which travels through space
Comforter: quilt; duvet
Common: held in unison; normal
Commotion: noise; tumult

Communicate: exchange words or ideas
Companion: partner
Compared: held up to in an effort to judge or form an opinion about
Compliment: say something nice to or about; words of praise
Computer: a programmable tool that performs mathematical computations
Con: scam
Conspire: work together
Contain: hold within
Continue: extend beyond; keep going
Contradictory: opposite; inconsistent
Convention: general practice; what's normally accepted
Cook: to heat food
Cool: slang for good, hip, interesting, exciting; moderately low in temperature
Cop: slang for police officer
Cork: spongy bark used to stop or seal the opening of a bottle
Corny: odd; quirky; cheesy
Cost, costs: amount of money required to buy
Could: alternate tense of can
Countdown: counting in decreasing order
Countless: a large, unknowable number; more than a person can count
Country: a foreign land
Couple: a pair
Course: see "of course"
Cow: an animal consumed in the form of beef in America; an animal worshiped in India
Crawl: move on one's hands and knees; to move across the ground like a bug

Creating: making; manufacturing
Crime: a violation of the law
Crook: thief; someone that steals
Croon: sing in an affected manner
Cross: go from one end to the other
Cruella: the evil woman from *101 Dalmations*
Cry: shed tears
Cuando: Spanish for when
Cupid: the Roman god of love often represented by an angelic boy with wings and a bow and arrow
Cur: a lowly sort; a mixed breed dog; a mongrel
Curd: see "bean curd"
Curse: a negative spell; on oath of condemnation
Cursing: swearing
Cut: see "made the cut"
Cute: attractive in a non-threatening way
Dammit: a mildly profane curse
Damn: condemn; used for emphasis; see "give a damn"
Damned: cursed
Dance, dancing: what non-repressed people do when they hear music; to move rhythmically
Dangerous: potentially harmful
Dare: challenge
Darker: less light; more mysterious
Date: based on a calendar, how we refer to a day; a social encounter, typically between two mutually attracted people
Day: a period of time between sunrise and sunset; a period of time approximately 24 hours long, during which the Earth rotates 360 degrees
Days: see "these days"
Dead: exact; not alive

Deadly: lethal; terminating of life
Dear: special one; cherished
Death: the absence of life
Decided: chose; determined; made up one's mind
Decirte: Spanish for to say to you
Dedicate: to declare something is for someone or some purpose
Deep: the opposite of shallow; profound; low; meaningful
Defeat: beat; come out on top of one's enemy
Definitely: surely
Del: Spanish for of (the)
Delib'rately: "deliberately"–on purpose
Delicious: good tasting
Delight: joy; pleasure
Delightful: enjoyable; pleasant
Demanding: challenging; difficult
Dense: thick; stupid
Deny, Denying: refuse to allow; discredit
Desire: lust; craving, wishing
Desperate: intense; up against the wall and having to win
Despite: notwithstanding
Destined: designed by fate to happen
Details: the particulars, the individual facts
Devotion: the application of something (time, energy, love) to something or someone
Dickinson: Emily Dickenson–American poet from the mid-19th century
Did: past tense for do
Didn't: contraction for did not
Die: lose life
Difference, different: not the same
Difficulty: challenge
Digs: verbal abuses

Dinner: the evening meal
Direction: the way something is going
Disbelief: lack of belief
Discern: figure out
Disgrace: something to be ashamed of; something out of favor
Disgusts: hatred; to cause a feeling of hatred
Dish: the plate food is served on
Dive: enter into
Do: make happen
Doctor: medical or other professional with an advanced degree
Does: present tense for do
Doesn't: contraction for does not
Doggerel: bad poetry
Dogs: more than one member of the canine family
Doing: alternate tense for do
Don't: contraction for do not
Done: finished; over
Door: opening; entrance
Dork: lame person
Doubt: uncertainty
Down: beneath; below; under
Downright: surely
Downtown: often the city center
Dramatic: stunning; capturing of human interest
Draw: use to inspire; take
Dresses: puts on clothes
Drift: float
Dripping: soaking wet
Drive, driven: force executed in a direction; what we do to cars; to move
Driven wild: made crazy, usually in a good way

Drop: fall from
Drugs: substances, usually taken internally, that alter human beings for better or for worse
Drum: a musical instrument upon which people beat in order to produce sound
Dumb: not smart
Duress: hardship; difficulty
During: occurs in the same period of time
Duty: obligation; task
Dying: running out of life
Each: one of two or more; every
Ear: the organ that allows us to hear, if we use it
Earn: merit; deserve
Earthly: being of the third planet from the sun
Eating: consuming food
Eight: the number between seven and nine
Elaborate: complex and thought out
Elated: very happy
Eliot: T.S. Eliot–a famous American and English poet from the early 1900's
Else: different; other
Else's: belonging to else
Emotion: human feelings, like happiness or sadness or anger
End: terminal; final
Endless: without termination
Enemy: opponent
Engage: enter into conflict with; grab the attention of
Engines: source of power
Enough: sufficient; an adequate amount
Enter: come into; go into
Entierren: Spanish for bury
Erotic: sexy; arousing
Error: mistake

Es: Spanish for it is
Escape: get away; to go somewhere different
Especially: used for emphasis, to isolate and differentiate
Ethereal: heavenly
Eve: according to many, from the Bible, the first woman
Even: to a higher degree; at the same time; exactly; equal or identical
Event: occasion; thing to do or attend
Eventually: in the end
Ever: at all times; at any time
Every: each and all
Everybody: all people; each person
Except: save for; but
Excitement: energetic happiness
Exerting: making effort
Exist: to be
Exotic: rare and prized
Experienced: having done much in life; been around the block a few times
Exported: taken away, like to another country
Express: state; say in words
Eye, eyes: the organ we use to see
Eyebrows: the hair on the ridge above the eyes
Face it: realize it
Face, faces: the front part of the head, has the mouth, eyes and nose
Fact: a statement of truth
Fails: does not succeed
Fake: not real
Fall: lose your footing; trip or drop down
Famous: well-known
Fans: people who really like something
Far: a long way away

Far and wide: all over the place
Fart, farts: the gas that comes out of your butt
Fascinating: awesome; spellbinding; able to capture one's attention
Fast: at a high rate of speed; quick
Fate: that which you cannot avoid; what's going to happen; destiny
Faults: imperfections; problems
Favorite: most preferred
Fear, fears: being afraid; apprehensive; really worried
Feed: give food to; nourish
Feel, feeling, feels: touch; to sense, often emotionally
Feet: the bottom part of the leg that touches the ground
Fell: past tense for fall
Felt: past tense for feel
Feminine: female; womanly
Feroz: Spanish for fierce
Fetus: an unborn baby
Few: not many, more than one
Fight, fights: battle; go up against
Fighted: a word I made up meaning fought
Filled: comprised of
Final, finally: the end; last; terminal
Find: locate; discover
Fine, fine: good; pleasant
Finish: stop
First: 1st; earliest
First rate: be just right; what the doctor ordered
Firsts: a word I think I made up meaning more than one first (if that's possible)
Fit: be the right size for
Fit the bill: be what's ordered; be just right for
Flashforward: move ahead; the opposite of flashback

Flatter: say nice things
Flick: movie
Flight: a trip through the air
Floor: the part of a room that is beneath our feet
Flor: Spanish for flower
Fly: to travel through the air
Fog: heavy moisture in the air, like very low clouds
Followed: trailed behind; came after
Fool: a crazy person, one easily tricked
For: used to indicate amount, destination, purpose, recipient
Foreign: from another place
Forever: eternity; never-ending
Forget: fail to remember
Form: type
Formal: really nice and proper
Fort: a protected building
Fossilized: really, really old
Found: located; discovered
Four: the number between 3 and 5
Fox: a crafty, wily, furry animal
Fragrance: aroma; smell
Frantically: in a hurried and crazy manner
Free: doesn't cost anything
Freud: Dr. Sigmund Freud—Austrian psychologist from the late 1800's to the early 1900's. Inventor of the concept of the id, ego, and superego; psychoanalysis; and other fun stuff like the notion of the conscious and subconscious mind
Friend: a person you share things with, whom you can trust
Frog: an amphibian that jumps
Frogette: a word I made up meaning female frog
From: used to indicate the origin, source, or starting point

Frost: Robert Frost–American poet from the late 1800's to the mid 1900's
Fun: a good time
Funny: makes you laugh
Fur, furry: soft hair that grows on the bodies of many animals
Furrows: scrunches up; creates a fold in
Fused: joined together
Future: what comes next
Fuzzy: made of soft, really short hair
Gal: girl
Game: a contest
Garden: a plot of land for growing vegetables, flowers, plants
Gauge: measure; determine
Gay: happy; homosexual
Generate: create; make
Gently: with tenderness
Gestation: pregnancy
Get, gets, getting: obtain; come by; understand; to have
Giggling: laughing
Ginsburg: Allen Ginsburg–American poet from the mid to late 1900's
Girl: young female
Girl's: belonging to the girl
Give: offer; transfer from one person to another
Give a damn: care
Glad: happy
Glance: take a look at
Glasses: spectacles; devices which improve poor eyesight
Glee: extreme happiness
Glide: move across a surface with little friction
Glory: renown; fame; praise

Gnome: a little person from fantasy
Go, goes, going: move; start
God: the almighty and powerful ruler of the universe…
    according to some
Good: kind; helpful; useful
Got: past tense (or weird version) for get
Grace: refined movement; effortless beauty
Grant: allow; offer; give permission
Gray: somewhere between white and black
Gray matter: nerve tissue in the brain
Great: really good; impressive
Green: the color you get when you mix yellow and blue
Greenish: sort of green
Griot: an African poet or storyteller
Groan: make noise when exerting strength; moan
Grow, grows: get bigger
Growls: makes a low, guttural sound
Grub: slang for food
Guess: try to figure out; supply answers that you think
    may be right
Guide: leader
Gun: a weapon that shoots bullets
Habit: repetitious behavior
Had: past tense for have
Hair: the thread-like things that grow out of a human head
Hand, hands: the end part of an arm where the fingers are
Happen, happens: takes place; occurs
Happy, happily: feeling good
Hard: difficult; challenging; with force
Has: variation for have
Haste: quickly; with speed
Hate, hates, hating: dislike; despise
Have, having: own; possess; are required

Haven't: contraction for have not
He: pronoun for a male
Head: the part of the body that contains the brain; go towards
Hear: interpret sound, typically by way of the ear
Heart, Hearts: the organ that pumps blood; the metaphorical center for human emotion and caring
Heat: warm temperature
Heavens: the skies above us; the place where some people think they'll go when they die
Hell: some unnamable thing below us; the place where some people think they'll go when they die
He'll: contraction for he will
Help: assist; give a hand to
Her: that female
Here: nearby; in this place; at this point; at this time
Here's: contraction for here is
High: up above; elevated
High school: the school attended by children ages 13 to 18
Hill: an elevated piece of land
Him: that male
Himself: that male only
Hips: the part of the body between the stomach and the thighs
His: belonging to him
History: the story of human past, like it or not. It's also most likely the story of human future, know it or not.
Hit: strike; beat
Hold: keep; maintain control of
Hold on: wait
Home: where one lives

Homer: ancient Greek poet, presumed author of the Iliad and Odyssey
Honest: truthful
Honor: high regard; esteem
Hope, hoping: to wish for something
Hops: jumps
Horny: aroused in a sexual manner
Hot: high in temperature; very warm
Hotter: higher in temperature
Hour, hours: used to mean the time; a unit of time
How: the way; in what way
However: but; nonetheless
Hugs: when you wrap your arms around something in an embrace
Human: Homo sapiens; people
I: the person who is speaking or writing
I'd: contraction for I would or I had
If: in the event that; on the condition of
I'll: contraction for I will
I'm: contraction for I am
Images: pictures or other visual representations
Immense: very large
Imperfect: not perfect; problematic
Imperfections: things that make something not perfect
Important: meaningful
Impress, impresses: to leave a favorable opinion
In: inside; within; located among; during; to a place
In store: waiting to happen; in reserve
Inaccessible: you can't get to it; too complicated to be easily understood
Incessant: doesn't stop
Infiltrate: move in, usually in secret
Innocent: not guilty; not corrupted

Inspiration: source of hope; stimulation
Instance: case; example
Instead: in place of
Intention: desire to make happen
Interstellar: among the stars
Into: to the inside of; against
Inviting: welcoming
Irony: the opposite of what is said; humor that arises from incongruity of meaning
Is: variation of be
Isn't: contraction for is not
It: that; this; the thing in question
Its: belonging to it
It's: contraction for it is
I've: contraction for I have
Jealous, jealousy: envious; when a person wants what another person has
Jerk: a mean person
Jiggling: bouncing and shaking
Joined: attached; merged together
Joy: happiness
Jumpy: prone to sudden movement
Juntos: Spanish for together
Jura: Spanish slang for police
Just: only; merely; proper; exactly
Just say no: the catchphrase for the "Say no to drugs" campaign
Justice: fairness; what's morally right
Keep, keeps: hold on to; preserve; maintain
Keys: the lettered components of a typewriter or keyboard
Kid: child
Kind: type; sort; example
King: un-elected rulers

Kiss, kisses, kissing: what two pairs of lips do when they touch; the ultimate in oral expression
Kneeling: spending time on one's knees
Know, knows, known, knowing, knew: to be aware of something; to understand something
LA: Los Angeles
La: Spanish for the
Lady: a woman
Lair: living space
Lame: bad; weak
Landed: hit ground (or some other surface) as a result of downward movement
Lascivious: lewd; perverse
Last: final; endure
Late, later: after the designated time; closer to the end
Laugh, laughs, laughter: happy noises
Launch: set loose; set in motion
Lay: to place on a surface; resting in wait
Lead: go in front of and steer
Learn, learning: understand; gain the knowledge of
Least: smallest amount; at the minimum; in any event
Left: went away; remaining; opposite of right
Legal: not against the law
Legs: the part of the body between the waist and the feet
Lejos: Spanish for far
Less: to a smaller degree
Lesson: something learned
Let, lets: allow
Let's: contraction for let us
Lids: coverings
Lie, lies: an untruth;
Life: existence; what you have if you breathe
Light, lights: brightness; illumination

Like: similar; such as
Line, lines: a path; something said, like dialogue; the edges of things have lines; a row of printed text
Lingered: remained
Lips: the protruding part of the mouth; the fleshy part of the mouth you kiss with
Literally: exactly what's written
Little: small
Live: exist in
Locale: a setting; where something takes place
Locked: kept in a protected place; stuck in a place
Long, longer: goes on and on
Look, looking: using your eyes to see; observing
Los Angeles: the city in California, USA where Mikka and Bones live
Lose: get lost; forget the location of
Loss: what you feel when you lose something
Lost: in an unknown location
Lot, lots: an amount
Loud: at a high volume
Love: what you feel when another person makes you forget yourself; fondness
Low: not high; below; to a small degree
Luck, luckily: fortune, for better or for worse
Lust: carnal desire; sexual desire
Lust's: belonging to lust
Lying: remaining at rest
Macho: manly
Made: past tense for make
Made the cut: qualified for
Magic: supernatural
Magnificent: really wonderful
Make out, making out: kiss

Make, makes, making: create; cause to occur
Man: male human
Many: more than a few
Marsi: Mikka's cousin
Masculine: male; manly
Matar: Spanish for kill
Matter: material
Matters: is important
May: could
Maybe: perhaps
Me: myself
Meal: what you eat, if you're lucky
Meanness: marked by ill-will or anger
Measure: what one does to determine size, weight, amount, etc.
Medieval: from the Middle Ages in Europe, about 500 CE (Common Era [AD]) to about 1700 CE
Met: was introduced to; came to know
Metaphor, metaphorically: a figure of speech in which one thing is understood as being similar to another
Metaphor's: contraction for metaphor is
Meter: the rhythm of poetry; poetry itself
Method: the technique
Mi: Spanish for my
Might: meaning it's a possibility
Might've: contraction for might have
Mikka: the woman to whom these poems are dedicated
Mind: pay attention to; the brain or the thoughts in one's head
Mind's: belonging to the mind
Mine: belonging to me
Miraculous: supernatural

Mirth: laughing happiness
Missed, missing: not there; absent; without
Mixing: combining; stirring together
Moan: make a low noise, usually from pain or sorrow
Mock: make fun of; imitate
Mold: fungus; form from which models are created
Monkey: a primate, almost like a human, but with more hair
Months: periods of time comprised of about 30 days
Moon: the celestial body that rotates around the Earth
Moons: subordinate bodies in outer space
Morally: relating to what's right and wrong
More: in addition
Morning: the first part of the day, when the sun rises
Most: the greatest part in terms of size and/or amount
Motion: movement
Mountains: really big hills; raised areas of land
MTV: Music Television–a TV station devoted to music
Much: many; a large amount
Mumbling: talking in a very low voice
Muse: the inspiration for many poets, Muses come to us from Greek mythology
Muse's: belonging to a muse
Muy: Spanish for very
My: belonging to me
Myself: me and me alone
Mysteries: weird, unexplainable things
Nada: Spanish for nothing
Naked: without clothes
Near: close to
Nebulous: unclear; indefinite; like interstellar dust or clouds
Need: what is required; what you have to have
Neither: not one or the other
Nervous: worried; unsure what to do

Neuter: not masculine or feminine
Never: not at any time
New: recent; not old; different
News: information about what's going on
Nice: kind; caring
Night: what follows day
Nine-month: the typical duration for human pregnancies
No: negative; not one; not
No longer: not anymore
Nooks: secluded places
Normal: prosaic; typical; ordinary
Nos: Spanish for we
Not: in no way; negative
Nothing: not anything
Notice: see; perceive
Now: at this time
Occasionally: once in a while
Ocean: a large body of water, like the Pacific or Indian Oceans
Odd: different; not normal
Of: from; caused by; associated with; directed towards
Of course: obviously; certainly
Off: the opposite of on; used to indicate position; manner; direction; purpose; movement; proximity; etc.
Often: frequently; many times
Oh: used to express a feeling, like of surprise or relief
Old: been around for a long time; been alive for many years
On: the opposite of off; used to indicate position; manner; direction; purpose; movement; proximity; etc.
Once: one time
One: the number between 0 and 2

Only: alone; sole; just; at the least
Oooh: used to express a feeling, like of surprise or relief
Opinion: a point of view; a belief
Or: used to mean the other; an alternative
Other, others: different than or different from
Otherwise: in a different way; also
Our: belonging to us
Out: in the open; away from something
Outbursts: sudden creation or explosion
Outlive, outliving: live longer; outlast; survive past
Outpace: move faster than
Outrageous: crazy; beyond what's acceptable
Overrated: not as good as people say it is
Overstand: meaning understand, but overstand implies knowing instead of believing
Page: a piece of paper, as in a book
Pain: hurting; suffering
Painted: colored with pigments
Paper: wood pulp fashioned into a material upon which we can write or draw
Paradise: the perfect place to be
Paradox: a contradiction
Paraphernalia: the things that go with something; personal belongings
Parker: Dorothy Parker—American poet from the first half of the 20th century, known for her sharp wit
Part: a section; a small amount of a larger whole; the role an actor plays
Pass the time: spend time
Passed: gone
Passes: words used to romance
Past: history; what happened before; beyond

Patiently: rest without struggle or discomfort
Pay: give money to
Pedantic: bookish; like a boring teacher
Pee, pees: go to the bathroom; urine
Pen: a writing instrument using ink
Penalty: punishment
People: humans
Perhaps: possibly
Perish: death to
Perk: benefit
Pero: Spanish for but
Perspiration: sweat
Pesky: annoying
Pheromones: chemicals emitted by humans (or animals) that affect behavior in other humans (or animals)
Piercing: poking a hole through
Pillow: a soft rectangular object that many people rest their heads on when they sleep
Pills: drugs
Pinche: Spanish for darn or damn
Piss: anger
Pits: as I use it, "armpits"–the underside of where the arm meets the body
Place: an area; a location; a position
Plastic: fake; artificially made
Plath: Sylvia Plath–American poet from the mid-20th century
Play: amusement; happy diversion; what you do when you participate in a game
Playmate: someone to play with
Pleasant: nice
Please: to make happy; to be willing to do
Pleasure: enjoyment

Plucks: pulls in order to remove
Pocketknife: a short, portable blade
Poem, poems, poetic, poetry: words put together in such a way (usually with meter and rhyme) to evoke meaning and feeling
Poops: goes to the bathroom; defecates
Pop: squeeze until something explodes
Por: Spanish for for
Possible: able to happen
Pound: hit with force
Practice, practiced: repeat in order to improve
Prefer: like better
Preserving: keeping; maintaining
Press: touch; make contact
Pretty: attractive; appealing
Prevaricate: lie
Price: how much something costs
Prick: a small hole made by piercing
Prim: proper; straight-laced; not corrupt
Print: put ink on paper
Problem: difficulty; a troublesome occurrence
Production: the manufacture of products; making things; what many workers do
Professor: a college or university teacher
Promise: pledge; state that something will or will not happen
Proper: suitable; right for that place and time
Prose: non-poetic writing; ordinary speech or writing
Prosper: do well; succeed
Pull: to tug at; to yank
Pure: free from faults
Purple: the color you get when you mix red and blue
Purposefully: having a purpose; having a reason
Purposely: on purpose; for a reason

Pursuing: going after
Put: place; make happen
Que nos entierren juntos: Spanish for "may we be buried together"
Query: question
Quest: search
Quick: fast; in a short amount of time
Quite: rather; completely; actually
Race: a group of people with common traits, like skin color; a competition where time is a factor
Rage, rages: anger
Rain: water drops that fall from the sky
Rapper: a person who raps; a singer of hip-hop songs
Rat: a furry rodent with a long tail
Rate: a quality level
Rather: preferably
Reach: to be able to grasp
Reaction: response
Read, reading: to look at and try to understand the meaning of
Ready: prepared
Real: not fake; actual
Realize: figure out; understand
Really: truly
Rearranging: moving around; putting in a different order
Reason: the justification; the cause
Recite: to say aloud, like a poem
Recommend: endorse; say good things about
Record: the written account of events
Recuerdeme: Spanish for remember me
Red: one of the primary colors, the one resembling the color of blood
Red-capped: wearing a red hat

Re-enter: enter again
Refine: to make more precise
Regalia: symbols of royalty or kingliness
Relief: feeling less pain; freedom from something
Remember: to not forget; to recall
Repeat: to do again or say again
Repent: to feel regret
Repose: rest
Reprehensible: that which should not be expressed; worthy of blame
Resist: hold back; oppose; don't go along with
Respond: reply; answer
Rest: the remainder, what's left over; cease moving, come to a stop
Restricted: limited
Return: come back; go back
Rhyme, rhymes: words that similar final sounds; poetry
Ride, riding: to be carried on; to sit on and move
Right: correct
Ring: a symbolic metal band that goes around a finger
Rise: move up
Risk, risking: to take a dare; to attempt a challenge
Roam: to wander about from place to place
Roamer: someone who likes to roam
Rockstar: a famous singer, or screamer
Romance, romancing, romantic: love, sex, allure, seduction
Romantics: as I use it, the poets who come from the Romantic Age of poetry, from the late 1700's to the early 1800's, including Wordsworth, Coleridge, Shelley, and Keats
Room: space; a walled off section of a building
Rose: a pretty flower

Rub: to move something, like a hand, across a surface
Rum: an alcoholic beverage
Run, running: like walking, only faster; move quickly through
Ruse: something done to confuse
Rush: move quickly, in a hurried manner
Sad: unhappy; down; blue
Safe: secure; out of harm's way; under no threat
Said: past tense for say
Sail: to move under power of the wind, usually in a boat
Sails: the large sheets that allow a boat to be driven by wind
Same: identical; similar
Sanrio: the company that makes "Hello Kitty" and "Badtz-Maru" toys
Sappy: cheesiness; lameness; almost sickening warmth and good feeling (I use the adjective as a noun just so that it rhymes)
Sass: clever, sometimes disrespectful speech
Satisfaction: happiness; contentedness
Saturday: the day of the week between Friday and Sunday
Save: keep in a safe place; preserve
Saw: past tense for see
Say, says, saying: speak; communicate
Scared: afraid
Scent: odor; aroma; something detectable by the nose
School: where people go to get a formal education
Scowls: makes a mean-looking face
Scribe: a professional writer
Sea, seas: a large body of water
Search: to look for; to try and find
Season: one of the major periods of the year, like summer, winter, rainy or dry
Secret: hidden; not for general knowledge

Seduction: to try and get someone to be with you romantically
See, sees: observes; detects with the eye
Seeking: looking for
Seem, seemed: appeared to be; felt like
Selfish: caring only about itself or oneself
Sensation: feeling; notion
Sense: meaning; to perceive
Serial: in installments (small portions at a time)
Service: when someone brings you something, like food
Session: a period of time during which something happens
Set: in place; a group of something, like songs
Setting: the place in which something happens
Settle: come to rest
Shall: synonym for will
Shame: feeling of guilt or embarrassment
Share, sharing: offering what you have to someone else
Sharper: more sharp; having an edge that can cut; smarter
She: her; that female
She's: contraction for she is
Shine: radiate light
Shivered: shook from the cold
Shops: buys things
Short: limited in height or length
Shortly: in a small amount of time
Should: ought; meaning obligation or duty
Shouldn't: contraction for should not
Shout, shouts: yell; scream; talk really, really loudly
Shower: like a bath, only you stand up and let water fall on your head and body
Shut up: "be quiet!"
Shy: not outgoing; cautious
Sick: unhealthy

Side: a surface of something
Siempre: Spanish for always
Sight, sights: something to see
Silently: without noise
Simmer: to cook, almost boiling
Simple, simply: easy; plain
Sin, sins: bad things humans do
Since: from the time when something happened
Sing, singing: voicing things in a musical manner
Singer: one who sings
Sisters: girls related to each other
Sit: rest in a chair; not standing
Skin: the organ that covers the body
Skinny: thin; no meat on the bones
Skull: the bones that make up the human head
Sky: the bluish thing above us; the upper atmosphere
Sled: a device for sliding, usually on snow
Sledding: riding on something that slides
Sleep: rest; what humans do when they are tired
Sliding: move smoothly over a surface
Slow: moving at a low rate of speed
Slumber: sleep
Sly: sneaky; secretly
Smack: make contact with
Small: little
Smart: intelligent; good thinking
Smell, smells: has the aroma of; detectable by the nose
Smelly: has a bad odor
Smile: raise the corners of a mouth as an expression of happiness
Smirking: smiling derisively
Snort: inhale strongly through the nose
Snow: frozen water that falls to the earth as white flakes

So: because; to an extent; therefore; as a result
Sole: only
Solo: alone
Solve: find the answer to; figure out
Some: a few; un unspecified amount
Somebody: an unspecified person
Somehow: in an unknown manner; for an unknown reason
Someone: an unspecified person
Something: an unspecified thing
Sometimes: every now and then; once in a while
Somewhere: in an unknown place
Song: musical composition; a poem
Soon: in a short amount of time
Soul: the spirit of a person
Sounds: is detected by the ear; noises
Soup: a liquid food usually containing meat and/or vegetables
Soy: Spanish for I am
Space: the area around something; the distant heavens
Spaceship: a vessel used to travel through space
Special: rare; of high value; different from usual
Special-tease: a word I made up as a pun for specialties
Spell: a magic saying
Spend: pay or offer in exchange; to use up
Spent: exhausted
Spit: saliva; the fluid in our mouths
Spy: see; look at stealthily
Squirrels: small, furry animals that live in trees
Stage: what a performer stands on in front of an audience
Stairs: steps one uses to climb or descend in between floors
Standing: up on feet; not sitting; remaining
Star, stars: a celestial body, usually visible at night
Stare: look at

Start, started: begin; commence
State: condition
Static: as I use it, conflict
Stay, stayed, staying: remain in place; don't move, don't change
Steer: control the direction of
Stew: a thick soup, usually with meat and vegetables
Stiff: hard; erect; rigid
Stinky: smelly; foul odor
Stocky: as I use it, like soup broth
Stomach: where your food goes after you eat; a principal organ for digestion
Stone: rock; hard material from the earth
Stop, stopped: come to a rest; cease moving; lack of motion
Store: see in store
Story: the retelling of events; fiction
Straight: not crooked; continuing in the same direction
Strange: odd; different; bizarre
Strength: force; power
Stress: tension
Stroke: caress with force
Strong: powerful; secure
Stronger: more powerful
Stuck: unable to move
Studies: ponders over and learns about
Stupid: dumb; not smart
Style: manner (of dress, of speech); look; design
Subconsciously: like in a dream
Subject: the theme or item that something is about
Such: the like; to a degree
Sukiyaki: a Japanese dish of stewed vegetables and meat
Sunday: one of the days of the week–in Christian lands, the day usually associated with rest

Suppose, Supposed: think of as true; to expect
Sure: positive; certain
Surprise: something unexpected
Suture: a seam, as in the line formed between skull plates
Sweep: carry away
Sweet: sugary in taste; nice
Swell: expand
Swim: move in water
Switched: exchanged; changed
Tails: the rear of most animals; what dogs wag
Take, Takes: require; grab; bring
Talk, Talks: converse; share dialogue with
Tall: vertically high
Task: duty
Tasting: detecting the flavor of
Teach: aid someone in learning
Tease: make fun of; flirt
Teenager: an adolescent from the age of 13 to 19
Tell: communicate something
Tengo: Spanish for I have
Tennineeightsevensixfivefourthreetwoone: 10, 9, 8, 7, 6, 5, 4, 3, 2, 1
Tequila: a liquor originating in Mexico made from the Agave plant
Terrier: a type of dog
Terse: curt; concise
Test: challenge
Tethered: tied to
Than: used to indicate the second part of a comparison
Thankful: grateful
That: the one referred to
That's: contraction for that is
The: used before a noun to denote a particular or specific

example or to designate which
Thee: old word for you
Their: belonging to them
Them: those people
Then: not now
Theory: ideas that may not be practical; abstract thought
There: away from here; that place
There's: contraction for "there is" or "there has"
These: the ones over here
These days: now; in this period
They: them over there
They'd: contraction for they would or they had
They're: contraction for they are
Thing, things: items; objects
Think, thinks: the process of generating ideas in one's mind; believe
Thinner: skinnier; less fat
Thirtieth: 30th; the cardinal number representing 3 x 10
This: the one right here
Though: except; but
Thought, thoughts: an idea in the mind; the product of thinking
Three: one plus one plus one
Thrive: do well
Through: from one side to the other; in the midst of
Throughout: across the whole
Throw: toss
Thrust: to exert force; to push
Ti: Spanish for you
Tight: firm; constricted; narrow
Til: contraction for until
Time: how we keep track of things that have a beginning, middle and end

Times: see at times
Timeship: a vessel for traveling through time
Tire: feel fatigue
Tired: exhausted
To: in a direction; towards; resulting in; concerning; in relation to; against
Today: this day; the present time
Toe: the fingers of your feet
Together: united; with each other
Tomatoes: a red fruit that grows on a vine
Tomes: long books
Tommy-boy: Mikka's cousin
Tonight: this night
Too: as well; also
Top: the highest point; the best
Toss: throw
Tousle: to playfully mess up
Trance: a dreamlike state
Transcend: to cross over; to go beyond
Transported: to be taken somewhere
Travel: to go somewhere
Treat: a reward
Tree: a tall plant, usually with a trunk
Tree-dwellers: people or animals that live in trees
Trip: stumble; fall; go from one place to another
Troubles: things that bother; things that cause distress
True: correct; straight
Try, Trying: attempt
Tu: Spanish for you
Tug: a little pull
Turn: revolve; alter; contort; twist; change to; make become
Turned: changed to; made become
TV: television

Twist and turn: slang for what's up ahead; the future
Two: one plus one
Two cents: slang for opinion
Umbrella: a personal folding device used to block the rain
Unclothed: naked
Undefinable: indescribable with words
Under: beneath; lower
Understand, understood: comprehend; get the meaning of
Unique: individually different
Unite, United: bring together; join
Unity: togetherness
Universe: everything known to man; space and matter
Unknown: not known; not understood; not perceived
Unless: if not for the fact that...
Until: before a time
Up: above; used for emphasis, as in "shut up!"
Upon: on
Us: you and I
Uses: functions
Value: price; worth
Vast: large; expansive
Vegas: short for Las Vegas, Nevada, USA
Ventura: Spanish for luck
Verse: a line of poetry; poetry itself
Versus: against
Very: extremely; particularly
Vessel: a container
Viene: Spanish for come
View: a way of seeing something
Vintage: from a previous era
Voices: the sound people make when talking
Void: an empty space
Wait, waiting: to be patient until something happens

Wake up: arise from sleep
Wanna: slang for want to
Want, wanted: desire; wish; lack
War: battle; armed conflict
Warm: to heat; mild temperature
Warning: cautionary signal; alert to danger
Was: past tense for be
Wasn't: contraction for was not
Waste: trash; the byproduct of human digestion
Wave: a ridge of water that crashes on the beach
Way: path; manner
We: you and I; all of us
Weather: changes in the pressure of the atmosphere
Web: what spiders spin; the world wide web
Web cam: a camera designed to record video for playback on the world wide web; also what Mikka called a really bad zit on my forehead one time
Well: good; skilled; in addition
We'll: contraction for we will or we shall
Went: past tense for go
Were: past tense for be
We're: contraction for we are
Weren't: contraction for were not
What: which thing; something unknown
What's: contraction for what is
When: what time; a time
Whenever: any time; every time
Where: what place; what location
Which: what one or thing; the one; any one
Whiff: smell a small odor
While: during; at the same time as
Whirl: spin
Whisper: speak at a very low volume

Whitman: Walt Whitman—American poet from the 1800's associated with a long white beard. Writer of *Leaves of Grass* and many poetic songs about American industriousness.
Who/Whom: what person
Whole: entire; complete
Why: for what reason
Wide: over a large area
Wife: a female spouse; a married woman
Wild: untamed; crazy
Will: used to mean future occurrence or probability
Wind: a gust of air; the movement of air
Window: on opening through which one can see
Wings: what birds and planes use to fly
Winter: the coldest season
Wish: to hope; an expression of desire
Wishing: hoping
With: accompanying
Within: inside
Without: not having something; outside
Withstand: put up with; survive through
Witness: to see something; someone who sees something
Womb: where a baby lives when inside its mother
Wondering: pondering; thinking about
Won't: contraction for will not
Wood: lumber; what trees are made of
Woods: forest
Wooing: courting; pursuing someone romantically
Word, words: a written or spoken symbol; the basis for communication
Work: labor; toil; effort; a job
Works: is effective

World: the place in which we live; the planet
Worn: aged; not new
Worse: not as good; inferior
Worth: of value
Would: past tense for will
Wouldn't: contraction for would not
Wrath: anger
Write, writing, written: to compose with language; to put words on paper
Wrong: in error; mistaken
Y: Spanish for and
Yawn: one thing we may do when we are tired, marked by the extreme widening of the mouth
Year, years: a period of time marked by the passage of approximately 365 days
Yearn: really want
Yes: an affirmative expression
Yesterday: the day before today; all or any days before today
Yet: nevertheless; up to now
You: the person being addressed
You'll: contraction for you will
Young: early in life; those who are in the early period of life
Younger: born more recently than
Your: belonging to you
You're: contraction for you are
Yourself: who you are
Zits: acne; pimples
Zygote: a fertilized egg

About the Author

Bones Kendall is really Evan Kendall, a professor in the English/ESL department at Los Angeles City College.

Understanding that most great poetry is hard to read, he figured he would bridge the gap with accessible and interesting poetry celebrating love. Poetry is what it is because it's not everyday prose, and poetry is good for your soul, and studies show that reciting it is good for your heart.

Originally, the glossary was started to help with the harder words, but then which words were hard and for whom? Better to do them all...

www.ingramcontent.com/pod-product-compliance
Lightning Source LLC
Chambersburg PA
CBHW061655040426
42446CB00010B/1753